# Shift Your Focus

## 30 DAYS TO CHANGING YOUR MINDSET... LIKE A BOSS

## Jackiea Brooks

ISBN: 979-8-218-51153-1

# About the Author

I am a 34-year-old woman who grew up in a small town between Port Norris and Millville, New Jersey. I was pregnant at 15 and had my first child by the age of 16. It was a journey, because at 16 you're still a child yourself. I worked as a bartender during that time while attending school to become a nurse. I struggled as a single mother while trying to fulfill my dreams, also making sacrifices for myself and my family.

In 2020, at the age of 32, I opened my own business, a boutique called Jayslayllc (www.Jayslayllc.net). Now, I'm a published author.

I've always been highly driven and had an ambition to want more out of life. With major and minor setbacks, I've somehow stayed focused and have persevered to better my life. My determination was to always show women that we can overcome anything if it's meant to be, regardless of the setbacks, if we believe in ourselves and remain consistent. Most importantly, we must train our minds to be smarter than our hearts.

Trust in God that things will soon fall into line with faith, hard work, and dedication. In this life, people will try to bring out the worst in you. Set healthy boundaries in your life so you can raise your standards. Remember, you're in control of your mind and your actions.

Hurt people hurt people who are hurt-able. Regardless of how the situation looks, stay 10 toes solid and you'll come out on top every time. Never do to them what they did to you, just BOSS up and keep your eye on the prize. Let your SUCCESS speak for you!

 **Jayslayllc Jackiea Brooks**

 **Jayslay_llc**

 **Ladyslay2020**

# Scriptures for the Next 30 Days

Matthew 1-3

Matthew 6:33

Psalms 3-5

Psalms 23:5

Psalms 118-25

Psalms 112:3

Luke 6:38

Luke 1:37

John 10:10

2 Corinthians 9:6-8

2 Corinthians 9:8

Romans 15:13

Romans 9:13

Romans 15:13

Deuteronomy 8:18

Deuteronomy 28:11

Proverbs 3: 9-10

Isaiah 41

# TO-DO LIST

start date

DAY : ___________________          DATE : ___________________

## Breathe /Clear Mind for 30 Seconds

☐ ______________________________________
☐ ______________________________________
☐ ______________________________________
☐ ______________________________________
☐ ______________________________________
☐ ______________________________________
☐ ______________________________________
☐ ______________________________________

**NOTES** ______________________________________
______________________________________

## What Is it I Want to Change?

☐ ______________________________________
☐ ______________________________________
☐ ______________________________________
☐ ______________________________________
☐ ______________________________________
☐ ______________________________________

# ( *Daily* ) SELF—CARE



## CHECKLIST

- ◯ MAKE YOUR BED
- ◯ TAKE YOUR MEDICATIONS & VITAMINS
- ◯ SKINCARE ROUTINE
- ◯ HEALTHY MEALS
- ◯ GO FOR A WALK
- ◯ CLEANING HOUSE
- ◯ WASHING CLOTHES
- ◯ LISTEN TO MUSIC
- ◯ HAVE A POWER NAP
- ◯ SOCIAL MEDIA BREAK

- ◯ TAKE A LONG BATH
- ◯ DO A FACE MASK
- ◯ CALL A FRIEND OR FAMILY
- ◯ MEDITATION
- ◯ WATCH A MOVIE
- ◯ CUDDLE A PET OR HUMAN
- ◯ TRY A NEW RESTAURANT
- ◯ MAKE TIME TO READ
- ◯ TRY A NEW RECIPE
- ◯ NO PHONE 30 MINS BEFORE BED

## WORKOUT

- ◯ CARDIO
- ◯ WEIGHT
- ◯ YOGA
- ◯ STRETCH
- ◯ REST DAY
- ◯ OTHER

## THINGS THAT MAKE ME HAPPY TODAY

## HOURS OF SLEEP ( Hours )

1   2   3   4   5   6   7   8

## WATER BALANCE ( Glass )

1   2   3   4   5   6   7   8

## MOOD

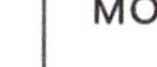

ANGRY   TIRED   SAD   GREAT   FUN

# DAILY MANIFESTATION

**I WANT TO MANIFEST:**

**MY PRAYER TO THE UNIVERSE:**

**VISUALIZATION:**

| I see | |
| I have | |
| I feel | |

**MY DAILY AFFIRMATIONS**

1. --------------------------------------------------------------------------------
2. --------------------------------------------------------------------------------
3. --------------------------------------------------------------------------------

**ACTION PLAN**

1. --------------------------------------------------------------------------------
2. --------------------------------------------------------------------------------
3. --------------------------------------------------------------------------------

# Well, Hello There!

You did not pick this book up by accident. It was purposefully placed for you. It's time to shift your focus, mind, body, and energy to greatness. This book is a book to read daily. Don't try and read it all in one sitting; allow yourself to complete the exercises. Each day, place yourself in the room/setting and dive in deep to shift your focus.

I'm proud of you first for wanting change. Second, for taking accountability to change. And last, simply for acknowledging it's time for change.

Don't be too hard on yourself for the next 30 days. Just remain consistent and remember to celebrate all your wins, big and small, whether they're a short- or long-term goal.

# Day 1 to Changed Behavior

Good morning, kings and queens! Today, take a moment to embrace where you are today. Don't think of all the things that are going wrong or that have gone wrong; instead, take a step back and first thank God that you aren't half of where or what you used to be. Take a moment to give yourself grace. Pat yourself on the back for the days you did not want to continue but you pushed through anyway. Take a deep breath: inhale deeply and exhale deeply. Do that for a course of 30 seconds to cleanse your mind.

Now that I have your attention, take some time to whisper to yourself:

- I am strong
- I am powerful
- I am worth my dreams
- I am capable of getting the job done
- I am intelligent
- My past can not and will not haunt me (control me)
- There is power in my words
- My thoughts will be positive
- I believe in me
- Abundance will shower my life (financially and spiritually, peacefully and easily)
- I am a magnet to life, peace, wealth, and elevation

I would like to take you on a journey with me to when it felt like my life was crumbling. The only thing I could think of was how and why I was going through so much, but as I continued to fight the battles, I began to identify the power in them (the lessons in each season). I began to appreciate the storms. Each time I gained new stripes, whether they were battle wounds or relationship pains, the lesson was in each step. Today, take a step back and appreciate the lesson. Know this situation can only harm you if you allow it. Everyone is dealing with something, but if you choose to be the victor instead of the victim, you will find the light at the end of the tunnel. Today, take some time to relax your mind. Do something you enjoy and take your mind off the people, places, and things that are troubling you. It just takes 30 minutes a day of your time. In this time, write down five goals that you want to accomplish in the next 30 days. Recommit to them daily.

# Take Some Time, Be Gentle with Yourself, and Recap

# Take Some Time, Be Gentle with Yourself, and Recap

# Day 2 of the Shift

Good morning, kings and queens! I hope you had a great nights rest and mind cleanse. Let's start the day by thanking God for waking us up this morning. That's the greatest opportunity. Thank God for an eased mind and a cleansed heart.

Take a moment to sit quietly for 30 seconds, inhaling then exhaling deeply and calmly. During this time, capture every moment that is holding weight in your life. Release it wherever you are. Call the name of the people, place, or thing that seems to be regularly clouding the space in your mind and then throw it out! Once it's released, you no longer owe it any power. This moment is very important because you have to be willing and ready to release your traumas.

Next, be grateful for the strength and courage to push forward. I'm so proud of you (change can be a scary thing), especially when the things you're choosing to walk away from are things you have seen in your lifetime or future. It's ok; don't get weary.

Remember, you have to take some L's to gain the Wins. Fai(L) = a first attempt in learning. Don't ever think you'll bypass that step in life. When we appreciate the lessons in the L, life seems to get a little easier. You learn to say things like, "Thank you, God, for the opportunity to take that L so I can know how to deal with different battles and handle them in a classier way. I no longer wear my scars. I no longer need validation from others to feel secure." Put your chin up and chest out!

Read the goals you wrote yesterday. Envision where you would like to be in the next five years. Start speaking manifestations out of your mouth: "Thank you, God, for my new Mercedes 2025 with leather heated seats. Thank you, God, for my newly-built 6-bedroom home with a 3-car garage and my new, loving husband." Be very specific. Another example is, "God, thank you for removing me from people, places, and things that NO longer serve my purpose. Please remove anything that is going to negatively affect my future." When you speak things into your life, sometimes the house comes down. It's ok, just be ready to rebuild, brick by brick, but this time with a solid foundation. Be the root, the foundations of the tree; the branches you grow will be solid in this season because you're seeing clearly in your thinking with a clean heart.

Go crush it today!

# How Are You Shifting this Season?

# How Are You Shifting this Season?

# Day 3 to Shifting Your Focus

Before you read this, I want you to repeat this step from yesterday: inhale deeply, close your eyes, relax your mind and body, then exhale through your mouth. Repeat this 3-4 times.

Today is important because you'll be going through all types of emotions with the changes and healthy habits you're putting into place. Don't get exhausted; don't even think about giving up. Don't be afraid of the changes. Don't be afraid of what's being left behind. Get out of your mind and out of your own head, thinking that things could fall apart. In fact, think of all the great things you've written on your list of things you're about to receive because you spoke it out of your mouth.

Today it is very important to be careful of what you entertain (people, places, and things). If you're not careful, you'll find yourself entertaining situations you're overqualified for. This will leave you exhausted.

Often, we go places we've outgrown or we'll open a door to a relationship we've already prayed away. In this season, there is no looking back. You can't run a race looking backwards. Keep your head straight and focused on the goals set before you. Anything behind you is a setback and holds no value in your future.

Today I want you to list:
- the people, places, and things that have caused you harm, mentally, physically, or emotionally
- the things that weigh you down
- the things that hurt your feelings continuously
- the things that hold no value
- the things that make you question
- the things that belittles you
- certain phone numbers/ social media accounts you need to block, unfollow, or mute

These are the things you tolerate and entertain and the reasons you're in your own head and second-guessing your potential. Anytime you find yourself repeating any of these cycles and undervaluing your worth, I want you to simply repeat this:

*I am strong. I am capable of living a peaceful life. I am learning daily. I am not what they say. I am the person God created me to be. I don't have to beg for love, friendship, or a spot at anyone's table. I will with hard work and dedication rebuild and reshape myself into the best version of myself. I am completely capable of being consistent to my goals and being cautious of my heart.*

Now relax and know this: you are enough.

Take the time to get some things done. Change your playlist to nice mellow music to set the tone. You got this. I'm so proud of you for putting forth the effort to change.

# Feed Your Focus
## Starve Your Distractions

# Feed Your Focus
# Starve Your Distractions

# Day 4
## Learn to Be Faithful to You

This is important. Many times, we put other people's importance over our own. We are all guilty of this. To some people, learning to put yourself first can seem selfish and unheard of, but truth be told sometimes you have to be selfish to get your mental health to a place where you're physically able to care for others. It's simply burnout from holding everything together.

Sometimes, people take a few days to step back and evaluate their lives so they can show up and be a better version of themselves. They do this so they can assist the next person. Self care is one of the main things people neglect because of the guilt or shame others may project onto them for giving themselves the self care they need. But it's ok. Think of it like this: when you're working a job and you're physically, mentally, and emotionally checked out for whatever reason, what do you do? You take a personal day or two, whether it's a sick day or vacation day, you take it. To be honest, you've earned the paid time off. Consider that the same way an employer owes you the days you've worked to be paid without actually coming to work. You owe it to yourself to have a self care mental health moment to be able to regain yourself without feeling guilty.

# What's Your Breaking Point?

# What's Your Breaking Point?

# Day 5

During this transition, it's important to keep an open, clear mind. When you need guidance and understanding, talk to God and not other people. Get comfortable with leaning on your own understanding!!!

Today is called **execution**.

Take  a moment to breathe. Relax your mind so you can think clearly.

Today is the day you shift your gears. We all want to be the boss and have a successful business, but at times it feels normal to settle in the place you are. Today, re-shift your focus and expand your horizons.

Today, you decide to not allow your current situation to dictate your destiny. If you can dream it, so long as you believe it, it's yours.

Today you decide not to settle.

Today you decide to be in control of the situation, especially if its changeable.

Today you decide to have multiple streams of income.

Today you become fearless if the chances of it not happening are greater or something going wrong

It's the shift of focus that makes it all come together.

We all say we want to be the first at something in our families but are you putting in the sacrifice? You need to know that during this time you will lose a lot of ships. (Relationships, friendships, business-ships, etc.)

Think of it like this: God put the vision in you. He didn't call you on a 3-way with other people. He installed the vision into you so YOU have to be unafraid of what could go wrong. Take the a leap and believe it's within you.

You can't tell a dream to a person who has never dreamed. You can't talk business with a person who doesn't own a business. You can't talk billionaire to a 100aire. It's time to open your eyes and take that leap on faith.

Buckle your seatbelt, its time!

In this season, it's about knowing and valuing your worth, raising the bar, and setting yourself up to be the Boss you are called to be.

Take some time today to learn new words, and when you don't understand something don't be afraid to ask a question to clarify.

Jot down 5 things you are putting into play for execution and stick to it. Baby, it's your time!

Baby, can you smell it? It's billionaire season!

# Mental Cleanse Is Therapeutic

# Mental Cleanse Is Therapeutic

# Day 6

Don't give up when you feel overwhelmed (go harder!). Now be mindful: I'm not saying keep pushing if you're burnt out. Overwhelmed simply means when things just seem like your hands are in a lot of pots as you're striving for success. Understand that nothing worth having is easy. You're allowed to take a day off but you're not allowed to throw in the towel and give up. That's never an option. Winners NEVER quit and quitters NEVER win. I speak these words to myself daily. So feed your focus and starve your distractions. This means you should give your time and energy to the things that nourish you spiritually, mentally, and emotionally, and starve anything that doesn't have the capability to assist your growth. If a plant doesn't have sunlight and water, it cannot grow. Start with the root which is you and be gentle with yourself.

You're allowed to mess up but you're not allowed to stay in the mess! It's time to take back control and get refocused. You've got this!

# Planning to Prevent Exhaustion

# Planning to Prevent Exhaustion

# Day 7
## Look Who's talking!

Who's on your phone feeding you info? Who's around you talking? What are you bringing in your mind from your surroundings?

Remember, when you're in the process of transition, you'll be tested. Not everyone has your best interests at heart. This is why its important to know who's in your ear during this season. Don't get tricked back into the people, places, and things (your Triggers). Triggers can make or break you.

For example, I picked out a casual outfit of my liking and attended a friends birthday party. I had the time of my life, posted a picture, and went about my Sunday.

I received a call Tuesday about the event stating someone was at work showing my picture and asking why would I wear that.

It's funny because you never know if you've changed until your hand is forced. By that point in the day I was in a great mood and about to attend boxing, but that phone call diverted my mind. I couldn't understand why they needed to talk about me. I didn't realize I had to get approval from the shaderoom.

Later, I couldn't allow the situation to die because the person who said it was a friend. I slept on it after the gym but got back up the next day and wanted war!!! I texted the person in a rage just to find out they weren't the person who said the comment. That person and I ended up having a very healthy conversation. She was able to see why I would be upset, and I could only appreciate her for being honest.

You can see how quickly my energy changed. I allowed a situation that shouldn't have mattered affect my day. Instead of me just telling the person I'd call them back, I RSVP'd to an IRRELEVANT SITUATION that didn't deserve my attention because honestly what does it matter what was said?

You say you want to be the first billionaire in your family and the head of an eco company, yet you look down to address a confused fan (don't do that). In this particular moment, I should have looked in the mirror and said, "Of course they would be a critic. Look at who I am. I am the chosen one. I was built for this." Rejoice over the downplay because God already choose you. The validation from a individual who's lashing out due to misery and uncertainty shouldn't even be frowned upon; it should be appreciated.

I love you. Go crush it today!!!

# The Power in Words

# The Power in Words

# Day 8
## Stop Shrinking for Acceptance

Do you ever feel like you're too much for some people? Do you ever feel like you have to dim your lights for certain relationships to work?

Today, look in the mirror and speak these words to yourself:

I am the light in any room I walk into<br>
I am a game changer<br>
I am a leader<br>
I can only grow<br>
I will never shrink to fit in<br>
I have self-awareness<br>
I am better than yesterday<br>
I will not get offended when something no longer serves my purpose<br>
Anything that belittles or devalues me is not for me

If everyone were the same, no one would be different. What makes a \$100 bill stand out from a penny? It has more value, you can do more with it, and more people prefer to have it versus the penny, right? So view yourself the same. You are who you are. People value you, they prefer to book you instead of another company, and they prefer to have your products. If you don't ultimately see yourself as the iconic person you are how do you expect anyone else to believe it?

Every day from this day forward, I pray you view yourself through the eyes of greatness. Any and everything you touch and do will be full of abundance. When you walk into a room, the energy from your presence will shift the room. People will gravitate to you with positivity. "Wow, what's she drinking? I want some of that!" (The only thing you drank was a cup of hot coffee!) Because you have the juice. you show up differently.

Remember: show up and show out. Repeat this daily and never dim your lights.

# Build Your Confidence

## Who/What Lowers Your Value?

# Who/What Raises Your Value?

# Day 9
## Be Careful of Who God/the devil Sends

Breathe deeply. Inhale and exhale, baby, because this step is very important.

When you're trying to transition and focus you have to be careful because you become lonely simply by thinking about the what if's and the maybe it could have been this. But it's important to understand that if it's for you, it won't be a battle; it will be easy.

During this time, some days may be better than others. Your phone may be a little dry. Your social and love life may seem a little off, but it's ok to spend a little more time with yourself. The devil has a way of sending distractions from the thing you're wanting and speaking to. You must be extra careful because he can only damage what you allow him to access. God does send people, but the devil sends people too.

I'll give you an example. I used to have a friend who I had nothing in common with besides talking about our hurts and past trauma. During this season, I was broken and he was too. Things ended up going to THE next level with us. Now, the entire time I knew this wasn't the person for me because of the way he treated me. You know that old saying, "You have to teach them." I just don't see the good in that. I hated the way he spoke to me. He had no gentle touch; he was just rough and angry. I don't believe a man should ever be comfortable watching a woman work harder while they reap benefit, but I allowed it!

Remember, the devil will send his people when he thinks you're weak. He will attach leeches to you. I believe you truly don't know a person until he has nothing. Character is something that can never be tainted. It's like DNA, once it's yours, there's no changing it.

I prayed myself away from that entire situation. When you are free from a situation, it's beyond foolishness to return to that very same thing. It had you out of alignment in a season of looniness. Your thoughts will have you thinking a fool has changed. In all reality, most people just learn how to hide it better, but I always say if you want the truth about someone, make them upset and back to square one they will go.

How do you know when it's time to guard your heart? Your body is weak, you feel sick and tired daily, you're always upset and angry, you're arguing, and the household is in a uproar. You have childhood trauma, or something triggers you. What matters most is the source you turn to when you're hurt. The bite, the pain, can kill you slowly if you're not careful.

Yes, God will send people at the right time. But be careful because the devil will line his people up too. The devil wants you off balance and out of alignment. Stay on track and focus. This is your season already – it's yours!

Be careful what you turn to when you're vulnerable. Pay attention to what you fill your mind with when you're vulnerable. When you're shook, you're open. Fear will have you moving oddly (you become fearful of everything).

# Don't Get Distracted
# By the Test

# Don't Get Distracted
# By the Test

# Day 10
# Table talk
# (Be ok with Positive and Negative Correction)

Pull up a chair. This is for the bosses and bosses only.

At this point in your life and career, you should want to surround yourself with likeminded people. If you're running a business, your friends should also have businesses. Now I'm not saying you can't communicate with people who don't have a business, but what I am saying is your circle is a reflection of you. There's no way you can hang out with people who pout every weekend and think you're not going to lose some form of focus eventually.

This season is very important because you shouldn't be the smartest and most successful person in your group. Be ok with allowing people on a higher level than you to pour into you.

I had a woman say, "Jay, what's up with you lately? I see you haven't been going to the markets and going to events like you used to."

At that moment, I'm like, "You're right." I didn't get upset and think negatively. It was like a little check to get me refocused. It's very therapeutic when you're getting better acclimated to the next chapter in your life to attend healthy dates and seminars with people who want the same. The table is full of millionaires. It's hard to talk money to people who are comfortable being hundredaires. Don't eat your own, but if you want more you have to surround yourself with more.

Speaking and manifesting is very important in this season. Control your thoughts and the company you keep, the phone conversations you engage in, and the places you hang out. Keep your chill times to a minimum. If you have time to chill, you have time to work and aim a step closer to your goal. This season isn't for distractions.

# Who's at Your Table Talking?

# Who's at Your Table Talking?

# Day 11
## Learning to Communicate

Communication can make or break any relationship. Some people communicate to respond and others communicate to listen. I strongly believe this has a lot to do with past traumas and current situations. If you're always the strong person, it seems others don't think you need a shoulder too. Because you're labeled the strong one, it may seem like a form of weakness when you communicate a cry for help. Help doesn't equal weak. This gets confused a lot of times and could make someone shut down. If you don't communicate your feelings and emotions, how does anyone know? If you continue to move and groove like nothing is wrong, how can you expect others to just guess? I had to learn this the hard way. It caused a lot of darkness because I felt like, *Well, why don't they know how I'm feeling?* Communication can be a lack of understanding on both ends, but if the person hurting had just communicated their emotions, the situation could have been addressed. On the other hand, there is the fear of not having a safe place to vent. This alone could make a person break completely down and never open up to a soul.

I have something better for you. If you're ever feeling down or emotionless, learn to journal. Writing your feelings and emotions is another tool that can allow you to destress in a safe space.

I strongly recommend learning how to get on your knees and speak to God. He's the only person Who can turn any situation better, so why not turn to Him?

In life, you have to learn how to speak up about things that are causing harm to yourself. If you never tell a person something they said hurt your feelings, how will they ever know? If you don't like chicken and the chef makes chicken, are you just going to eat it because you don't know how to communicate? Some may say it's a totally different situation but it's actually the same thing. In this season, learn how to communicate your wants and needs without feeling as if it's the wrong thing to do. You have the right to decide what you choose to participate in. This season, communication is key. Hold eye contact, keep your head high, speak gently, and stand on it.

# How I Currently Communicate

# Do I Listen to Hear or Hear to Respond?

# Ways to Change How I Respond

# Day 12
## Don't Look Back

This phase is really funny. People always say you're acting differently when you want to change, but when you work so hard for a better life, you must change into a better version of yourself.

Instead of getting upset when they say that, take it as positive criticism. You're showing improvements. Even though the person saying it is probably being critical, you have to see the good in it.

For example, if you want to be a millionaire, you will need to be around people who make you uncomfortable. Why? Because in order to grow, changes have to be made. Comfortability and change don't mix.

It's good to have long-term relationships; however, some of your childhood friends have never even made it out of their neighborhood. How can you expect them to help you get to the next level? This is why it's healthy to meet new people.

It's also ok to move away if you feel you're unable to remain focused. You're not running away from a situation. Really, you're simply changing your surroundings. Your surroundings can play a major part in your growth.

If the people you hang around with have no ambition, no dreams, and are afraid of taking risks and making changes for success, they could project their fears onto you and keep you bottled in and small-minded. Remember, birds of a feather flock together.

If you're in a community where being a business owner isn't normal, it may seem like you think you're better when in all reality you just want better. The best way to mess up your future is to rely too much on your past.

Sometimes, people feel bad for making it out. It's like a success guilt. This is the fastest way to fail.

# Things I Need to Let Go Of

# Things I Need to Let Go Of

# Day 13

Don't forget to take a rest day!
During this season, it's important to take rest periods
when you're working so hard and aiming for greatness.
Remember to take a moment for yourself, whether it's
exercising, taking a long walk, or simply reading a book.
Practice healthy eating habits.
One day out of a two week period is dedicated to rest.
This means:
no housework,
no work,
no overthinking.
Just YOU time to collect your thoughts.
You will be surprised by how therapeutic this is.
It's like a recharge to the body.
Be gentle with yourself. Change takes a lot of courage and a lot
of mental stability, which can be exhausting.
I'm so proud of you for staying consistent and not giving up.
You're putting yourself first for once.
Smile and embrace yourself!!!
Let's Gooooooooo!

# Things That Relax Me (Happy Place)

## Places I Enjoy that Relax My Mind

# Books I Enjoy For Relaxation Time

# Day 14
## Worrying Only Makes Things Worse

Do you ever sit and think to the point that you overthink? I think we all have, but what do you do when you feel like you've worried yourself and you're restless from the worry? Worrying doesn't always have to be bad. There are normal and abnormal stressors.

There is a thing called eustress, a normal stress. It could simply be the need to get the laundry completed by a certain time, running the kids around, or not forgetting a doctors appointment.

On the other hand, you have chronic stress, the things that are out of your control such as a death in your family, overdue bills, or a bad doctor's report. These negative stressors are called distress. They are the things that constantly worry us, whether they're situational or from the things we have encountered in our lives. Even though they are different, they still cause worry and doubt.

Each day, you have to take a breath before beginning it. Instead of listing all the things you have to do and tasks that need to be accomplished, try to attack it from a different point of view. Write the things that need to be completed, cross out the things you have completed, and give yourself deadlines. Try planning your day the day before so when you wake up you're on a schedule. Leave a little time in between tasks in case something happens so you don't become flustered when surprises come up. Life on the daily will throw you things, good, bad, or indifferent. You have to adjust with life's stressors without becoming easily overwhelmed.

You've got this! Give yourself some grace as you tackle the tasks. Don't allow the tasks to become unbearable. This causes burn out and defeat. You are bigger than that.

# Eustress (Normal Stress)

## Acute Stressors

# Chronic Stressors

# Day 15
## Boundaries

Create healthy boundaries to maintain your sanity. This right here can make or break a person

Do you ever feel as if you're not being walked over, you don't fit in? Or as if so long as you're doing what the other person asks, the relationship is in good standing? It's very therapeutic to set healthy boundaries so you don't feel underappreciated.

A person can only tolerate and stand for what they allow. For example, let's say it's the holidays and you know you have to be around certain members of your family who always seem to put you down for whatever reason (you not being married, not having children, you talking a certain way, you always wanting to look nice or "bougie," you wanting nice things). This can be a stressful situation and cause anyone to feel anxious or not even want to go.

Setting healthy boundaries in this situation could be before the conversation even starts. "Hi, uncle/auntie! No, today we're not going to speak about my life or the things I'm not doing to your liking. Let's talk about sports or the weather." If that doesn't work, simply walk away and don't participate in that conversation. Walking away from the conversation sets the tone of healthy boundaries as to what you will or will not speak about. All these things take time, but if you stay consistent about what you truly believe, people will gravitate to you and respect the boundaries you put up. In the event they do not, it's ok to be conscious of your boundaries without feeling guilty about it. 💋 Take some time to write some healthy boundaries you want to put in place moving forward.

# My Healthy Boundaries

# My Healthy Boundaries

# Day 16
## My Thoughts

It's time for a mental check-up! Where are you mentally today? Have you made progress or are you falling off track?

If you are falling off track, why?

What can you do to realign and shift your focus?

# Realigning and Refocusing

# Day 17
## How to Kill a Big Dream

The best and quickest way to kill a big dream is to tell it to a small-minded person. This doesn't discriminate as to who that person can be. Sometimes we think the most support should come from our loved ones, but half the people who are successful will tell you they didn't get there with the people they knew. Whether family or friends, never box yourself into believing the best support has to come from people you know. In some cases, a person will see someone close to them working their passion. Because that person may have been afraid to follow their own dreams or they may not have had the courage to believe in themselves, they will project a lot of disbelief into the dreamer. If it comes from the correct person, the dreamer may believe they aren't capable of being the thing they once believed they could. Put your trust and faith in God with everything you do. He will direct you in the correct path so you won't have to turn to others for validation on what you should or shouldn't do. Lean on him for understanding and everything will fall into place. If it's for you, no one can stop it. The only person who can stop your dream is you. If it's God's will you may delay it, but it will soon return at the correct time.

Continue to believe and dream. It's winning season!

# Dreams/ Goals

# Dreams/ Goals

"Impossible
only exists if
you never try.
Believe and
execute
@Jayslay

# Day 18
## Stop Reliving the Same Hurt

Life hits everyone differently. Everyone has different traumas, different pain, different sacrifices, how they grew up, or were raised. Our views in life are all different. The one thing that is the same is pain. In life, you can't escape pain, and a lot of pain comes from the people you love the most. Never allow yourself to become so hung up on the things that happen, especially if you've already prayed about it, repented to God, and have spoken about it to the participants to address the situation that's causing the hurt. You don't have to live forever in a choice you had to make for whatever reason. I always say this from a friend I used to communicate with: hurt people hurt people who are hurtable. Stop allowing people to make you relive trauma through guilt or shame. It's important to forgive yourself. Once you ask God for forgiveness, that's when you move on from it. It's easy for people to bring up all the bad you've done to distract the focus from their own pain and suffering, but remember, some people love being sick. They love the attention your pain brings to their life. You can't decide to be better and choose to be the person who carries the knife. You be the better person who chooses to turn your pain into power and help others heal from their hurt and past traumas. You never know who can gain healing from something you were able to grow from.

Chin up! You're only a victim of your past if you agree to stay there. Today, make the choice to push forward. Flowers bloom after bad weather, so after the storm it's your time to shine!

# How I'll Let Go of Hurt

# How I'll Let Go of Hurt

# Day 19
## Re-evaluation

Lord, I'm so thankful for where I am. I'm even more grateful for the strength and courage to continue, even with tough times and betrayal, even when I feel like the world is against me I continue to fight. Gratitude, now that's a great word.

By now, I'm sure you, just like myself, have had some bad days and may have even been beating yourself up when you feel you're off track. But honestly, you're where you're supposed to be. The fact that you've taken the initiative to change is always a great first step.

I have been walking around being beyond grateful. I'm thankful for my friends, my family, my coworkers, my business partners, and so on. Even if every relationship isn't where it needs to be, every challenge helps shape your character. My character has been tested on so many levels that I can be only grateful for growth and understanding which helped shape my character!

These last few weeks have taught me so much about how to communicate differently. I don't respond the way I used to. I know how to control my thoughts, my mouth, and my emotions. It's hard, but when you learn how to allow the universe to control you, you become one dangerous beast!

The best lesson life has ever taught me was this: apologies are most granted when the other person can't hear, feel, or appreciate it. The people who appreciate you when other people want to purposefully hurt and demolish your character, are those who see the greatness in you. Don't allow the defeat of someone's opinion taint your character. I'm so proud of you, not for what you've been through, but what you've grown into and elevated from. Remember, always take the time to be grateful, because you aren't who you used to be. I love you, guys!

# Self-Reflect

# Self-Reflect

# Day 20
## Learn How to Adjust in Any Situation

No one wants to be the new person. Have you ever noticed that a new person always has to go through the extra hoops and hurdles? Blah! But think of it like this: being the new person allows you to seek new opportunities and better relationships. After all, first impressions are everything.

This is a perfect time to bless the unknown with your talent. You don't know how talented someone is until you talk to them.

But then you have the territorial types who don't like change or new things. That's ok, learn to adjust and work around them.

In any situation, never allow a person to determine your level of growth by their ignorance of character or their disapproval.

Every day is a day to self-reflect and give yourself confidence so you can be in a place of victory even in a what appears to be a place of utter defeat.

Remember, defeat is only complete if you yourself to throw in the towel. You never know what you're capable of if you assume the outcome is failure. If you attempt and fail, you've learned from the thing that didn't work, but if you attempt and quit because of disapproval, you'll forever live in a state of doubt.

Be easy on yourself. You've got this! Believe, execute, and repeat daily.

# Things I Need to Adjust

## How Can I Adjust?

# What's Stopping Me from Adjusting?

# Day 21
## Stress Kills Faster than Any Disease

Have you ever been so overwhelmed that you feel as if your head will explode? You're to the point of exhaustion and your headache is so heavy from trying to prove to your loved ones how much you truly love and care. Everyone sees what you don't do, but they never see how much you actually do? If you take nothing else from me, understand this: you will kill yourself trying to make people value you. Out of every time you were there, if a person wants to go against you, the only thing they will remember is the time you weren't there, or the time you couldn't, never the time you tried the best you could. This gives so many people an opinion about you, like what they would do if they were you, or how you should handle a situation, when in all reality they wouldn't be able to stand tall like you do after carrying your battles.

You only get one life, and there is no blueprint to how you should or shouldn't be. Everything is trial and error. Be kind to yourself because you are human.

This world can be so cruel if you allow it to be. You can't control things that are out of your control, you just have to learn how to adjust. Otherwise, you'll allow everything to stress you out to the point of depression. If you knew how quickly people forget about you when you die, you would stop allowing people, places, or things to control you with how they believe you should handle things. You don't owe anyone an explanation for you wanting better and choosing peace over dysfunction. It's easy to remain the same and be "normal." It takes courage, strength, and power to change narratives and put healthy boundaries on your life. Do not allow people to run over you, friends or family. You are human and you have a right to be treated as a person with feelings. You do matter! 💋

# Healthy Habits to Handle Stress

# Positive Words For Myself

# Day 22
## The People You Need in Your Life

When you're in a transition phase, you need people in your circle who
- will hold you accountable
- correct you when you're wrong
- let you know when you're deviating from the plan
- will pour into you equally

Transitioning can seem very hard if the people, places, or things around you are constantly trying to make you focus on the things you're trying to free yourself from. You have to be stronger than your weaknesses. Your weakness can be your mind making you feel like what you're doing is a bad thing. People may stop inviting you places, stop calling you, or start hanging with other people. These are just clarifications that you're a step closer to your breakthrough. If you want to run a business, it's best to be around people who can't go out every weekend because they need to show up early to conduct their business. It's hard to stay on track if you're sleeping in from partying the night before. Another example is if a person is ok with going to work and just coming home, that's not compatible with sometime who's trying to touch the world with their voice or talents. Have you ever met a person who has all of these hopes and dreams but they fear getting started or staying consistent? This is why it's important to be around a circle that will keep you accountable: "Hey, how's the book coming along?" No one can motivate you to do something you don't wish to do; however, it's very hard to be around people who are winning if you ultimately do not want to bring winning to the table.

This season can make or break a person. If you're weak, you may fall into thinking that you're the problem, when in reality you have to change what used to be your daily circle of friends. Removing an influence doesn't mean you're mad at the people, places, or things. It simply represents changed behavior and being consistent.

Remember, time is valuable. Giving too much time to the wrong audience can make or break a person.

You're transitioning your mind to be the best version of yourself. Why not be particular with whom you offer to spend it with?

# Evaluating My Circle

## Who Decreases Value?

# Who Adds Value ?

# Day 23

What are you feeding your body? You only have one body. At a certain age, you'll start to notice that you aren't able to do things like you were once able to do them. It's ok. You just have to do more self-care and appreciate your body. What you consume plays a major role in your thinking, attention span, energy level, and the way you feel as a whole. Take some time to create healthy eating and lifestyle changes to put into place for a healthier life. Some examples are: instead of eating out, do meal prep. Instead of chips, eat fruit. The food you consume is very important. Remember to drink water. Many people think they don't have time for this or they forget.

Also, you can exercise for at least 30 minutes a day, whether you're taking a walk, jogging, doing yoga, or stretching to move your joints and relieve some tension.

Remember to rest so your body isn't overworked and exhausted. Create healthy patterns and set schedules to stick by to help you stay on track. For example, my goal is to be in bed by 9:30-10pm so I can be up by 5am to write. That way, I have an open, clear mind. If I stick to the same goal, I will train my body to be sleepy at that time every day.

Here are some healthy tools and tips so you can overcome the overwhelm of your daily routine:

- Be kind to yourself
- Eat healthy
- Stay hydrated
- Exercise
- What do you give your energy to?
- What do you entertain?
- Do you get enough rest in between tasks?
- Are you a procrastinator?
- You got this!!! Start practicing better daily habits and watch how quickly your life changes!

# Healthy Lifestyle Changes

# Healthy Lifestyle Changes

# Day 24

Whoahhhh! Does life seem to be giving you a run for your money?

Listen, what worth having is easy? Everyone has a different story; it doesn't mean one takes priority over the other. It just means they're the cards you were dealt. I strongly believe that if we would stop looking at everything as if it were a battle and started having gratitude for the life lessons, things would move more smoothly with less heartache and pain.

I listen to a podcast. Instead of the speaker complaining about what they have been through and the troubles that came up in their day, they begin to speak, "Thank you, Lord, for my journey. Thank you for a mind to be able to overlook the negative things. Thank you for allowing me to notice things I've outgrown. Thank you for giving me a vision when I lost that job and I was blessed with the career I prayed for."

We are often defeated when things don't move at our speed, but that's the best thing about faith. It has a way of just sneaking up on you but always at the right time.

So on a daily basis, instead of looking at what happened, what you may have done wrong, how things used to be, or what could be different, take that same time and energy and create the life you envision and are praying for. Replace all your doubt with gratitude for this battle and redirection. The shift begins with your mind, and it allows you to shift your thinking, so don't get weary. It's time to exhale and let faith activate you.

# How Am I Feeling Today?

# How Am I Feeling Today?

# Day 25

Isn't it funny how you're only important to others when you're needed? Or are you considered selfish? Any of you going through your children telling you how much you were never there for them and how the other parent does much more?! Let me be the first to tell you: be gentle with yourself and give yourself grace and some gratitude. Don't allow the people you love to make you feel guilty for refusing to be a walking doormat. DON'T EVER LOSE YOUR POWER! You owe it to yourself to set healthy boundaries and not allow people to constantly downplay you because you no longer participate in being used and abused. Remember, if things are only going great when you're pleasing others, remove yourself immediately. Eventually you'll be at a state of burnout from always being a yes person because you're too afraid your NO will cause you to no longer be appealing to the person you don't want to disappoint.

If you take nothing else from this book, remember to never give up on yourself. Never allow the defeat of life to make you feel as if you haven't given your best, even when most days you had nothing to work with. It's ok to push forward and choose to no longer be a victim of your past. Stop allowing the hurtful words spoken by others to make you feel humiliated to the point you want to throw in the towel. You owe it to yourself to go extra harder in those moments because you are important, you do matter, your presence is worth more then just money, and you deserve genuine love. You're allowed to have a bad day, but you're not allowed to bring it to the next day. Remember, you can only try so much but think of it like this: when a battery is used, eventually it runs out of power and dies out. Stop allowing others to drain the life out of you to the point where you're lifeless. Don't allow your problems to change the person you are on the inside; just change what you give your energy to and what you allow your mind to to focus on. Today it's time to stop sleepwalking on yourself. Wake up! Know that your life is valuable and know that you deserve to have good people around you.

# Remove the Door Mat

# Remove the Door Mat

*Words* have power. They can *make* or *break* a person, a relationship, a *nation*. Choose them wisely.

# Day 26

Take a moment to close your eyes. Breathe. Inhale and exhale gently, relaxing your mind. Imagine yourself living your dream. Visualize your name on that building or business letterhead. Picture yourself signing the closing deal on the new home you've been praying for. Picture yourself clicking on your online banking account that's filled with millions so you can overly bless the people you love. Time is very important because change requires constant reminding and self-reflection. Remember to recognize and celebrate what you've done.

This season is important. As you're reflecting, things may seem odd, because the people, places, and things you once thought would climb the ladder with you may or may not be around, and that's ok. Some seasons you have to be ready for things to change and rapidly. Other seasons are therapeutic when you go through them alone so you can hear one sound and one sound only. As you're reading your bible, find scriptures that pertain to your situation, and remember to take notes and be silent so you can hear God speak through you in the best way. This time is personal, because you need to be able to understand the difference it's asking for is understanding. During this time, most people won't understand that you have to be ready to deal with the negative feedback that comes with walking your own journey. Remember: all you need is an ounce of faith, an ounce of hustle, and a heart that believes you deserve it. Then you just take off. God did not bring you this far to leave you. Even if it seems like everything is falling apart, you are exactly where you're supposed to be. Smile! Things are coming together.

# Reflection Time

# Reflection Time

# Day 27 Planning
# MONTHLY GOALS

## JANUARY

## FEBRUARY

## MARCH

## APRIL

## MAY

## JUNE

## JULY

## AUGUST

## SEPTEMBER

## OCTOBER

## NOVEMBER

## DECEMBER

# DAILY GRATITUDE

/    /

TODAY I'M FEELING

POSITIVE AFFIRMATIONS

TODAY I'M GRATEFUL FOR

1
2
3

SOMETHING I'M PROUD OF

MORE OF THIS:

LESS OF THIS:

MY FAVORITE MOMENT THE DAY

TOMORROW I LOOK FORWARD TO

# Day 29
# *Monthly* BUDGET PLANNER

## 📅 MONTH

| JAN | FEB | MAR | APR | MAY | JUN | JUL | AUG | SEP | OCT | NOV | DEC |
|-----|-----|-----|-----|-----|-----|-----|-----|-----|-----|-----|-----|

## ☷ INCOME

| DATE | DESCRIPTION | AMOUNT |
|------|-------------|--------|
|      |             |        |
|      |             |        |
|      |             |        |
|      | TOTAL:      |        |

## 🛍 EXPENSES

| DATE | DESCRIPTION | AMOUNT |
|------|-------------|--------|
|      |             |        |
|      |             |        |
|      |             |        |
|      |             |        |
|      |             |        |
|      | TOTAL:      |        |

## ⭐ SUMMARY

| TOTAL INCOME | TOTAL EXPENSES | TOTAL SAVING |
|--------------|----------------|--------------|
|              |                |              |

## ✏ NOTES

# Day 30
# *Monthly* BUDGET PLANNER

## 📅 MONTH

| JAN | FEB | MAR | APR | MAY | JUN | JUL | AUG | SEP | OCT | NOV | DEC |
|-----|-----|-----|-----|-----|-----|-----|-----|-----|-----|-----|-----|

## ☰ INCOME

| DATE | DESCRIPTION | AMOUNT |
|------|-------------|--------|
|      |             |        |
|      |             |        |
|      |             |        |
|      |             |        |
|      | TOTAL:      |        |

## 🛍 EXPENSES

| DATE | DESCRIPTION | AMOUNT |
|------|-------------|--------|
|      |             |        |
|      |             |        |
|      |             |        |
|      |             |        |
|      |             |        |
|      | TOTAL:      |        |

## ★ SUMMARY

| TOTAL INCOME | TOTAL EXPENSES | TOTAL SAVING |
|--------------|----------------|--------------|
|              |                |              |

## ✎ NOTES

# DREAM

# PLAN

# EXECUTE

# REPEAT!

*The perfect time is now!*

Work
HARD
Dream
BIG
Never
GIVE UP

# Notes

# Notes